Vanessa Hudgens

ABDO
Publishing Company

A Big Buddy Book
by **Sarah Tieck**

VISIT US AT
www.abdopublishing.com

Published by ABDO Publishing Company, 8000 West 78th Street, Edina, Minnesota 55439.

Printed in the United States.

Coordinating Series Editor: Rochelle Baltzer
Contributing Editors: Heidi M.D. Elston, Megan M. Gunderson, Marcia Zappa
Graphic Design: Maria Hosley
Cover Photograph: AP Photo: Mark J. Terrill
Interior Photographs/Illustrations: AP Photo: Tammie Arroyo (page 25), Stephen Chernin (page 15), Jeff Christensen (page 27), Imaginechina via AP Images (page 27), Daniel Ochoa de Olza (page 26), Chris Pizzello (page 5), Denis Poroy (page 28), SC Johnson/Bob Riha, Jr. (page 11), AP Images for Fox/Matt Sayles (page 21), Paul Skipper (page 12), Chris Weeks (page 12); Getty Images: WireImage for Ruth C. Schwatz and Co., Inc./Gary Gershoff (page 7), FilmMagic/Bruce Gilikas (page 19), Arnaldo Magnani (page 29), Jordan Strauss (page 17), FilmMagic/Michael Tran (page 23), Kevin Winter (page 13); iStockphoto/tonyoquias (page 8).

Library of Congress Cataloging-in-Publication Data

Tieck, Sarah, 1976-
 Vanessa Hudgens / Sarah Tieck.
   p. cm. -- (Big buddy biographies)
 Includes index.
 ISBN 978-1-60453-121-3
 1. Hudgens, Vanessa Anne, 1988- 2. Actors--United States--Biography--Juvenile literature. 3. Singers--United States--Biography--Juvenile literature. I. Title.

 PN2287.H737T54 2009
 791.4302'8092--dc22
 [B]
                          2008011383

Contents

A Rising Star

Vanessa Hudgens is an actress and a singer. She has appeared in television shows and movies. Vanessa is best known for starring in *High School Musical*.

Vanessa played Gabriella Montez in *High School Musical*. Gabriella is a shy, smart student.

Oregon

California   Nevada

Salinas

PACIFIC OCEAN

Los Angeles   Arizona

N
W   E
S

MEXICO

US®

Family Ties

Vanessa Anne Hudgens was born on
December 14, 1988, in Salinas, California.
Her parents are Gina and Greg Hudgens.
Vanessa has a younger sister named Stella.

The Hudgens family is close. Greg and other family members often attend events with Vanessa.

Manila is a modern city. It also has many beautiful historic buildings. Vanessa dreams of someday visiting Manila.

Did you know...

Vanessa's father was born in the United States. His family is Irish and Native American.

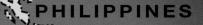

PACIFIC OCEAN

Manila ☆

PHILIPPINES

SOUTH
CHINA SEA

N
W E
S

A Proud Family

Vanessa's mother, Gina, grew up in Manila. Manila is the capital of the Philippines. People from the Philippines are called Filipinos.

Vanessa was born in California. Yet, she calls herself a Filipina. She is proud of this part of her family history.

A Young Actress

People first noticed Vanessa's talent when she was very young. She liked acting and singing.

At age eight, she began appearing in community **musicals**. She was in shows including *Cinderella*, *Carousel*, and *The Wizard of Oz*.

Did you know...

Vanessa is trained as an opera singer. She also plays piano.

Vanessa can sing, dance, and act. This is called a triple threat. These skills help her get more jobs.

Vanessa's costars in *Thirteen* included Evan Rachel Wood *(left)* and Holly Hunter *(right)*.

Vanessa **auditioned** for a television commercial and got a part. This was her first **professional** acting job. Soon Vanessa moved to Los Angeles, California. There, she began trying out for television shows and movies.

In 2003, Vanessa got her first movie part. She played Noel in *Thirteen*. The next year, Vanessa appeared in *Thunderbirds*. She learned a lot while working on these movies.

Vanessa and Brady attended the opening of *Thunderbirds*. Brady starred in this exciting adventure movie.

Did you know...

Actor Brady Corbet appeared with Vanessa in both *Thirteen* and *Thunderbirds*.

Vanessa also began appearing in television shows. In 2002, she had a small part on *Still Standing*. Vanessa appeared on *Quintuplets* in 2005. In 2006, Vanessa acted in *Drake and Josh*. She also had a part in *The Suite Life of Zack and Cody*.

Vanessa's popularity grew. Soon, she began appearing on shows such as *Total Request Live*.

School Days

Vanessa briefly studied at Orange County High School of the Arts in Santa Ana, California. Students in grades 7 through 12 attend this school. They prepare for jobs in television, music, dance, and other arts.

In addition to work, Vanessa spends time helping others. She attended the 2007 Power of Youth Benefiting St. Jude event in California.

As Vanessa got more acting jobs, she missed a lot of school. So, around seventh grade, she began attending school at home. This is called homeschooling.

Vanessa's parents were her teachers. This allowed her to travel and work as an actress.

Did you know...

Many famous young actors were homeschooled. Raven-Symoné, Elijah Wood, and Hilary Duff all studied with private teachers.

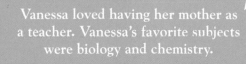

Vanessa loved having her mother as a teacher. Vanessa's favorite subjects were biology and chemistry.

Big Break

In 2006, Vanessa **auditioned** for a Disney Channel movie called *High School **Musical***. She got one of the starring parts! Vanessa used her singing, dancing, and acting skills to play Gabriella Montez.

Vanessa and Zac have won Teen Choice Awards for their work on *High School Musical*. Each winner receives a special surfboard.

High School Musical first appeared on the Disney Channel in 2006. No one expected it to be a big hit. But, it was an instant success!

Vanessa and the movie's other stars became famous. In 2007, they appeared in *High School Musical 2*. This movie was very successful, too.

In 2006 and 2007, Vanessa traveled the world with High School Musical: The Concert. She and the other stars performed songs from the first movie.

High School Musical

High School **Musical** and *High School Musical 2* are very popular. They are two of the Disney Channel's most successful movies. The first movie won an **Emmy Award**. This is a big honor for a television program.

The cast has appeared in magazines and on television shows. Fans can purchase High School Musical products. These include clothes, toys, albums, and DVDs.

Monique Coleman, Corbin Bleu, Ashley Tisdale, Zac Efron, and Vanessa starred in the High School Musical movies.

Making Music

After completing work on *High School **Musical***, Vanessa's career took off. She wanted to do more with music. So, she recorded songs for an album called *V*. The *V* stands for variety and Vanessa. This album was **released** in 2006.

Vanessa looks up to singers Alicia Keys *(far left)*,
Christina Aguilera *(left)* and Celine Dion *(above)*.

"Whisper" and "It Just Feels Right" are two of the songs on Vanessa's second album.

Buzz

In 2008, Vanessa appeared in *High School **Musical** 3: Senior Year*. She again played Gabriella. This movie first appeared in theaters, instead of on television.

Music and acting are both important to Vanessa. In between making movies, Vanessa works on her albums. Her second album went on sale in 2008. Vanessa has a bright **future**!

In 2008, Vanessa worked on a comedy called *Rock On*. She and Gaelan Alexander Connell filmed scenes in New York City, New York.

Snapshot

⭐ **Name**: Vanessa Anne Hudgens

⭐ **Birthday**: December 14, 1988

⭐ **Birthplace**: Salinas, California

⭐ **Home**: Los Angeles, California

⭐ **Appearances**: *Still Standing, Thirteen, Thunderbirds, Quintuplets, High School Musical, Drake and Josh, The Suite Life of Zack and Cody, High School Musical 2, High School Musical 3: Senior Year, Rock On*

⭐ **Album**: *V*

Important Words

audition (aw-DIH-shuhn) to give a trial performance showcasing personal talent as a musician, a singer, a dancer, or an actor.

Emmy Award an award the Academy of Television Arts and Sciences gives to the year's best television programs, writers, and actors.

future (FYOO-chuhr) a time that has not yet occurred.

musical a story told with music.

professional (pruh-FEHSH-nuhl) working for money rather than for pleasure.

release to make available to the public.

Web Sites

To learn more about Vanessa Hudgens, visit ABDO Publishing Company on the World Wide Web. Web sites about Vanessa Hudgens are featured on our Book Links page. These links are routinely monitored and updated to provide the most current information available.

www.abdopublishing.com

Index